HOMEMADE CAT FOOD & RECIPE COOK BOOOK FOR BEGINNERS

Complete guide on preparing home delicacies and treats with over 15 recipes for a healthy and happy cat

Sylvia Ross

TABLE OF CONTENTS

CHAPTER 1 4

   INTRODUCTION 4

      Why Make Homemade Cat Food? 5

   THE BENEFITS OF HOMEMADE CAT FOOD 8

   SAFETY CONSIDERATION 12

   Nutritional requirements for cats..16

CHAPTER 2: Understanding Cat Nutrition 19

   The role of protein, fat, and carbohydrates in a cat's diet 23

Chapter 3: Homemade Cat Food Ingredients 28

Chapter 4; basic Equipment and Tools for Homemade Cat Food 43

Chapter 5: Basic Homemade Cat Food Recipes 47

    Chicken and rice recipes 47

    Tips for Making Homemade Cat Food 53

    Turkey and Spinach recipe 59

    Vegetarian Cat Food Recipe 63

Chapter 6: Advanced Homemade Cat Food Recipes 66

    Homemade cat treats 72

CHAPTER 7 80

    Special Diet Cat Food (for allergies, kidney disease, etc.) 80

Chapter 8; Feeding Guidelines and Tips 87

    How much homemade cat food to feed 87

    How often to feed 90

Mixing homemade cat food with commercial cat food 91

Common mistakes to avoids 93

Follow basic food Safety 95

Size matters 97

Chapter 7: Tips for Transition 100

Getting your cat to love Homemade food 100

Getting your cat used to home-cooked meals 103

Veteran transition consultant 107

Conclusion: Making Homemade Cat Food for Healthier, Happier Cats .. 109

Copyright @ Sylvia Ross 2023

Without the author's prior written consent, no portion of this book may be duplicated, saved in a database form, or transmitted by any technology, including electronic, photocopying, or other methods.

This book's material and recipes are offered only for educational and informative reasons for you and are not meant to be a replacement for veterinary professionals' recommendations given, diagnoses, or treatments.

The content in this book is correct and current as of the time of publishing since the author and publisher have taken great pains to assure that.

Before making any dietary adjustments to your cat, the reader should speak with a veterinarian or veterinary nutritionist to ensure that the advice and recipes on here are suitable for their own specific pet cats as the reader is entirely responsible for making this/any determination in this guide book.

CHAPTER 1

INTRODUCTION

Why Make Homemade Cat Food?

You only want the best for your feline friend if you truly adore cats. You need to make sure your pet cat are happy, healthy, and well nourished. Making your own homemade recipe cat food is one method to start doing this.

However, given that you can readily purchase commercial cat food at the supermarket or online, why bother creating homemade cat food? The answer is very straightforward: homemade cat food offers several effective advantages that store-bought cat feed does not.

First off, making your own cat food at home gives you more control over the variety of the items and nutrients your cat consumes. You may not always figure/know what components are in commercial bought cat food, and some of them might not be the greatest competent for your cat's health. You can use fresh, nutritious, premium ingredients that are specially selected or made to satisfy your cat's nutritional demands when you make your own home made cat food.

Second, producing your own cat specialized food can be quite more affordable in the long term of keeping up the pace. Making your own cat home food enables you the owner to purchase materials in bulk and prepare bigger quantities of their feed, which will ultimately save you money over time of this practice,

Finally yet importantly, feeding your cat homemade cat food will be a gratifying and enjoyable experience for both you and your pet cat. We will examine the advantages of producing homemade cat food in this book; present a selection of recipes to test/try, and offer advice on how to cook these meals that are both balanced and very nourishing for your cat. By the time you finish reading this book, it will quite be knowledgeable enough to prepare wonderful home meals for your cat.

THE BENEFITS OF HOMEMADE CAT FOOD

1. Complete control over the ingredients in their meals: By making your own cat food, you

can ensure that your pet cat is receiving the greatest nutrition possible without the use of any hazardous additives or preservatives from commercial feeds.

2. Customized nutrition: Unlike commercial made cat food, homemade cat food can be produced to specifically satisfy the nutritional requirements you want for your cat.

3. Cost savings: Though preparing homemade cat food for them may cost more up front, but purchasing cooking materials in

bulk and producing bigger food quantities might result in long-term financial savings for you.

4. Better health: By giving your pet cat the appropriate amounts of all the nutrients they need, giving homemade cat food will boost your cat's general health and wellbeing. Over time this benefits can result in a healthier coat, better digestion, and more vigor.

5. Pleasant and rewarding experience: Making homemade cat food personally can be a rewarding and pleasant

experience for both you and your pet cat. It can help you two develop a closer relationship as time goes, especially working together to prepare meals and show your cat how much you value their health and well-being.

6. Avoid possible allergens: Some additives present in variety of commercially made cat food may cause allergies problems or sensitivities in some cats. You can solely prevent these possible allergies and make sure your cat is eating the right

food ingredients that is compatible with their system by creating your own cat food for them.

7. More variety: Homemade cat food will definitely provide your cat with a diet that has more diversity, which can help keep your cat more interested in its food and minimize boredom or pickiness habit.

8. Texture and consistency can be adjusted to better fit your cat's tastes and specific nutritional requirements when you make your own homemade cat food.

9. Better for the environment
10. Fostering deeper bonds and trust with you and your cat.

SAFETY CONSIDERATION

There are various safety factors/considerations that must be taken into mind while making homemade cat food in order to make sure that your pet can eat it, safe for them and that it is properly balanced enough.

Here are few crucial safety tips/points to always remember:

Before making homemade cat food, it is very crucial to speak/consult with your veterinarian to make sure the recipe you choose will suit your cat's nutritional requirements (especially allergic prompt cats)

1. Utilize premium ingredients:

To make sure the food you are making is secure for your cat to eat, use only *fresh*, premium components or ingredients. Utilize the use of fresh ingredients wherever possible rather than expired or tainted ones in their meal.

2. Good hygiene

To avoid germs or infection, practice excellent hygiene by thoroughly washing your hands, all utensils used, surface areas, and containers both before and after preparing your cat meal.

3. Cook meat thoroughly:

To eradicate any potentially hazardous germs in the meat as meat is a potential ingredients with high tendency to germs, be sure that all meat is properly cooked completely before using.

4. Selective components to omit:

Some substances/ingredients, including chocolate, onions, and garlic, are poisonous and not advised to be fed to cats. **Do not** include them in the food you give your cat or follow it on any recipes seen to try.

5. Maintain appropriate food storage:

To avoid spoiling of food, keep the homemade cat food in your freezer or refrigerator. It is crucial to carefully follow the directions given and make sure the recipe satisfies your cat's nutritional demands when utilizing a beginner's guide video/book to making homemade cat food.

Nutritional requirements for cats

Cats need specific dietary needs/requirements in order to maintain, avoid illness and improve their overall health and wellness for them. In this section of the guide: These are some of the essential components that a diet consisting of homemade cat food should have and be included in their meals:

- Protein

Protein is a significant nutrient; Cats must/should eat a diet high in animal-based protein since they are obligate carnivores in nature. Cooked meat (such as chicken, turkey, beef, lamb, and many more), fish, eggs, and dairy products are all excellent sources of protein for cats.

- Fat

To satisfy their energy demands, cats also need a diet/meal rich in fat. Cats can receive enough fat through animal fat, fish oil, vegetable oils and other sources in their meal.

- Carbohydrate

Cats do not need so much of carbs in their diet, although a modest bit of carbohydrate in it might provide them a little more energy. Carbohydrate meals like cooked rice, pasta, and potatoes are all excellent sources of carbs to give your cats.

- Vitamins and minerals

A balance of vitamins and minerals should also be included when making your homemade cat food. Providing a variety of fruits and vegetables or by adding supplementing will serve as vitamins and minerals to their diet.

Remember that homemade cat food diets can be quite challenging to perfect since they call for close consideration of the nutritional balance of the food given to your cat. As said, It is advised that you speak with a veterinarian or a veterinary nutritionist if you're interested in feeding your cat a homemade diet to make sure the food is fulfilling and meeting all of your cat's nutritional requirements.

CHAPTER 2: UNDERSTANDING CAT NUTRITION

The nutrition that cats need most

It is critical to comprehend cat homemade diet for the animal's general health and wellbeing's

Essential vitamins, nutrients, and they should be part of a cat's diet:

- Protein:

Cats need a lot of protein in their diet/meals to maintain healthy muscles and bones. At least 25[twenty five]% of a cat's diet should include protein, although certain cats may need even more amount of it.

- Fat:

Cats eat quite an amount of fats because they need them to absorb certain vitamins from them and as a healthy source of energy. Cats should eat a diet that is 10[ten]-15[fifteen] % fat.

- Vitamins and minerals:

Cats need a particular amount of vitamins and minerals in their food, which can be topped with supplements. These vitamins give nutrients include calcium, phosphorus, potassium, and the vitamins (A, D, E, and K.)

- Water:

Cats should always readily have access to fresh, clean water since they need a lot of it to be healthy and help for digestion.

Make sure the cat food you choose to make has a high percentage of protein from animal sources, such animal source like chicken, fish, or beef, by reading the ingredients list. Carbohydrates can be included but kept at minimum

Take note that certain pet cats could have particular nutritional requirements depending on their age, allergy, degree of activity they give off, or health. For instance, elderly cats need to eat less calories[fat] to avoid weight gain, and cats with renal illness needs to eat fewer proteins meals to relieve the strain on their kidneys.

The role of protein, fat, and carbohydrates in a cat's diet

The role of each nutrients [protein, fat and carbohydrate] in your cat homemade meals will be discussed in this part of the book.

❖ Protein

Since cats are known as obligate carnivores, which means they need a diet so rich in animal protein to survive; protein is a crucial food to make up every cat meals. Protein is essential for maintaining their muscle mass as well as for repairing and growing new tissue. The amino acids that is included in protein are necessary for the cat body to produce enzymes, hormones, and other essential compounds needed.

- ❖ Fat

For cats, as mentioned quite a lot in this book ,fat is a significant source of energy given and is required for the assimilation of several vitamins in their food . It helps your cat to keeping a lustrous coat and healthy skin. However, as we know too much fat in a cat's diet may cause obesity if not given with control, so it is important to keep an eye on how much fat is in their food.

- ❖ Carbohydrate

Cats do not need many carbs in their diet; certain cat meals may include them just as a source of energy to them, but the fiber from carbohydrates can assist them with digestion and reduce the risk of developing hairballs. However, consuming an excessive quantity of carbs might also result in weight gain and other health issues in cats over time therefore choose a cat food/diet with a low carbohydrate content.

❖ Vitamins and minerals

To maintain their general health and avoid common illness, cats need a particular amount of vitamins and minerals in their food/diet. Some of the most crucial nutrients are listed…:

- Vitamin A: Clear Vision, skin, and strong immune system health all depend on vitamin A.
- Vitamin D: Calcium and phosphorus absorption, both of which are quite crucial for the health of the bones, are aided by vitamin D.
- Vitamin E: Known As an antioxidant, vitamin E shields cells from deterioration.

- Vitamin K: Vital for blood clotting is vitamin K.
- Calcium: Vital for the health of your cat's bones, teeth, muscles, and nerves.
- Phosphorus: Supports development of strong healthy bones, teeth, and renal function.
- Potassium: Essential for healthy neuron and muscle function.
- Iron: For the creation of red blood cells, iron is required.

Maintain a well-balanced diet that supports your cat's health including enough protein, minimal amounts of fat and carbs, and the necessary vitamins and minerals needed. If you have any questions regarding your cat's nutrition and diet, it is vital to buy high-quality cat food/ingredients that complies well with these guidelines and to speak with a veterinarian or nutritionist.

CHAPTER 3: HOMEMADE CAT FOOD INGREDIENTS

Meat, poultry, and fish

Homemade cat food often contains most foods like meat, turkey chicken, and fish. Here are some advantages of each item as well as advice if adding them in the homemade cat food you make:

1. Meat:

For cats, meat is a fantastic source of protein to their meal as it has every necessary amino acid every cats need to keep their muscles, organs, and tissue in good and healthy condition.

Pork, lamb, beef, turkey, chicken, and other meats are all excellent choices to add for homemade cat food. Advised to fully prepare any meat used in homemade cat food in order to eradicate any potentially hazardous microorganisms in it, before giving it to your pet cat, you should also trim off any extra fat and bones to avoid injuries.

2. Poultry

Another excellent source of protein for your cats is poultry, such as chicken and turkey. It has less fat than certain other forms of meat, which is very good for cats that are prone to gaining weight quick. Before feeding your cat homemade cat food with poultry, make sure it is properly prepared.

3. Fish

Fish is an excellent source of healthful fats and protein for any cats as fishes contains omega-3 fatty acids, which helps lessen any inflammation and enhance the health of your cat skin and coat. Nevertheless, not all fish are good for cats, and some fish species have dangerously high mercury levels, which can be intoxicating. Salmon, tuna, and sardines are all good ingredients used for homemade cat food, while preparing these meals fully boil and remove any bones from the fish before using it in making your homemade cat chow.

While using these ingredients and more mentioned in this guide make sure that the meat, poultry, fish, and any ingredients used in homemade cat food are of excellent quality and devoid of chemicals or any form of preservatives. Checking that your cat's homemade food is balanced and fits their nutritional requirements/needs, you can also add additional items such as cooked veggies, supplements, grains, and vitamins.

A list of components of fish, meat and poultry ingredients;

- Duck
- Venison
- Rabbit
- Quail.
- Chicken
- Pork
- Beef
- Turkey
- Fish(sardines, tuna salmons)

Vegetables and fruits

1. Vegetables:

For cats, vegetables are a rich source of fiber, vitamins, and quite a number of minerals. They may also provide your cat's diet more texture and diversity. Cooked carrots, peas, green beans, and sweet potatoes are all excellent ingredients to use when making/preparing your own cat home food. Vegetables should be completely boiled and diced or pureed into tiny tiny bits making it simple for your cat to chew and digest when consumed in their meal.

2. Fruits:

Fruits provide cats with important vitamins, antioxidants, and fiber. However, there are certain fruits that should only be consumed in moderation or avoided completely since they are heavy in sugar content. Blue berries, apples, and bananas are suitable ingredients/fruits for making homemade cat food and should be used sparingly, diced or blended into tiny bits when preparing with them.

Choose or purchase fruits and veggies that are fresh, healthy and suitable for your cat's digestive system. Onions and garlic, for example, are poisonous to cats and should be avoided in their meal or as an ingredient. The fact that cats are obligate carnivores [meaning their body systems are designed to consume and absorb nutrition from animal-based protein sources in their food] is also significant to keep this in mind. As a result, high-quality meat, chicken, poultry or fish should make up the bulk of your cat's diet, added with vegetables and fruits serving as supplements.

Finally, before making any big dietary changes for your cat, speak with a veterinarian or veterinary nutritionist as they can assist you in coming up with a balanced and wholesome homemade food for your cat specified health.

The following list of fruits and vegetables are used to make homemade cat food:

- Sweet potatoes
- Carrots
- Green beans
- Peas
- Spinach
- Broccoli Kale
- Cauliflower Apples
- Blueberries

Starches and grains

1. Grains:

Cats get their energy and fiber from grains including rice, oats, and quinoa. However, cat's digestive systems are built to predominantly digest and absorb nutrition from sources of protein that come just from animals. As a result, grains and starch should be used sparingly in making homemade cat food and high-quality meat, chicken, or fish should make up the bulk of your cat's diet/meal.

2. Starch

Potatoes and sweet potatoes are examples of starchy vegetables that serve as a source of carbs and fiber in homemade cat chow/or as ingredients. Similar to grains, starches should only be included to a cat diet that largely consists of high-quality animal protein in moderation.

Because certain cats could be sensitive to the protein gluten, you should avoid using grains that contain it.

A list of grains and starches that can be used to make homemade cat chow is provided below:

- o Oats, brown rice
- o Quinoa Barley Millet

- Buckwheat Potatoes
- The sweet potato
- Lentils
- Chickpeas

Additives and supplements

To make sure that your cat is getting all of the vital nutrients they need to be healthy and active, you need to add supplements and other ingredients to your homemade cat food. The following are some typical supplements and ingredients included in homemade cat food, along with their advantages to your cat:

1. Minerals and vitamins

Vitamins and minerals are one nutrient that is very crucial for the general health and wellbeing of your pet cat. Vitamin A, vitamin D, calcium, and phosphorus are a few vitamins and minerals do well in cat's growth and health. You can find these nutrients, as they are available as supplements at most pet shops and online.

2. Probiotics

To encourage a healthy digestive tract and strengthen your cat's immune system, probiotics should be added to their feed. Probiotics are helpful bacteria that support the digestive tract's delicate microbial equilibrium in their diet and you can get them in powder or pill form.

3. Omega~3 fatty acid

Omega-3 fatty acids in homemade cat food supports healthy skin and fur as well as to advance general wellness of your cat. Fish oil, which is available in liquid or capsule form.

4. Taurine

Taurine is an amino acid that is crucial for the heart and eye health of your cat although it is naturally present in some sources of animal-based protein, you can offer taurine may as a supplemented nutrient with homemade cat food.

The following list of dietary supplements and food additives can be added to your homemade cat food:

- minerals and vitamins
- Probiotics
- A source of omega-3 fatty acids is fish oil.
- Taurine
- Lecithin
- metabolic enzymes
- Alcoholic yeast
- Glucosamine
- Chondroitin
- nutrients that assist joints

CHAPTER 4; BASIC EQUIPMENT AND TOOLS FOR HOMEMADE CAT FOOD

o *cooking scale*

When measuring materials precisely to cook, a kitchen scale is quite necessary, especially when dealing with meat and poultry substance. This tool guarantees that each meal your cat consumes has the proper quantity of each protein and other nutrients.

o *cutting board, butcher knives*

Cutting, chopping and preparing fruits, vegetables, and meats definitely needs a cutting board and sharp knives.

- *Food Processor or blending*

Meat, poultry, and fish needs to be ground into a fine consistency that makes it simpler for cats to digest after using a food processor or blender. Can also be used to purée fruits, vegetables, and not just meat.

- *mixing vessels/bowls*

For blending all of the components and ingredients, mixing bowls are necessary in making. The ideal choice advice is stainless steel since it is hygienic to use, clean and does not support microbial growth of any kind.

- *pans and pots for cooking*

To cook grains and starches ingredients like rice and potatoes, you will need to get a cooking pots and pans.

- *slow Cooker*

Fish, poultry, turkey and meat with other sort of ingredients are to be prepared in a slow cooker so that the nutrients in the ingredients are retained and the food is simpler for cats to digest and process.

o *Thermometer for meat*

To ensure that the meat, poultry, and fish used are cooked to a safe internal temperature of at least 165°F [74°C], a meat thermometer is necessary to carry this out.

o *Containers for storage*

To keep the homemade cat food cooked fresh and secure for consumption (especially when making in bulk), store it in airtight containers in the fridge or freezer after creating it for them.

CHAPTER 5: BASIC HOMEMADE CAT FOOD RECIPES

Chicken and rice recipes

Recipe 1: Chicken and Rice Cat Food

Ingredients:

Two (2) pounds of skinless, boneless chicken thighs

One (1) cup of diced carrots and 2 cups of brown rice boiled

One (1) cup of green beans, chopped

A tsp. of fish oil

One (1 tablespoon of dried parsley

One (1) teaspoon of dried catnip

Instructions:

1. Chicken should be cut/diced into tiny pieces and cooked thoroughly and browned in a skillet over medium heat. Set alone for cooling.
2. Brown rice should be prepared alongside per the directions on the box and then placed aside to cool.
3. Cooked chicken, cooked rice, diced carrots, and chopped

green beans should then all be combined in a big mixing dish.

4. In the dish, combine the fish oil, dry parsley, and dried catnip (if you using).

5. Serve right away to your cat or keep in the fridge for up to three [3] days in an airtight sealed container.

Recipe 2: Salmon and Sweet Potato Cat Food

Ingredients:

Two (2) cans of drained and mashed salmon, weighing 14.75 ounces each

Chop two (2) medium-sized sweet potatoes after peeling them.

Frozen peas, 1(one) cup

Coconut oil, 1(one) tbsp.

Oregano, dry, 1(one) teaspoon

One (1) tablespoon of dried thyme

Instructions:

1. Set the oven's temperature to 375°F (190°C).
2. On your baking sheet, scatter the diced sweet potatoes with the coconut oil(s). Bake for about 22~26 minutes, or until tender, in a preheated oven.
3. Frozen peas should be then boiled for 5[five]-7[seven]

minutes, drained out, and then placed away to cool off while the sweet potatoes cook.

4. Mash the tinned salmon fish in a large mixing basin/bowl and stir in the prepared sweet potatoes and peas boiled. Then Mix thoroughly.

5. Mix it all once more before adding the dried thyme and oregano to the bowl.

6. Serve right away to the cat or keep in the fridge for up to three (3) days in a closed container.

Recipe 3: Turkey and Vegetable Cat Food

Ingredients:

Two (2) pounds of turkey ground

Cooked quinoa, one (1) cup

One (1) cup of spinach, chopped

One (1) cup of carrots, chopped

Olive oil, One (1) tbsp.

One (1) teaspoon of rosemary, dry

One (1) tablespoon dried basil

Instructions:

1. The ground turkey cooked thoroughly and browned in a skillet over medium heat.

Afterwards set alone for the turkey to cool.
2. Quinoa should be prepared per the directions on the box and then left also aside to cool.
3. Combine the cooked ground turkey, cooked quinoa, adding chopped spinach, diced carrots in a large mixing dish.
4. Mix thoroughly with dried basil, dry rosemary, and olive oil in the same bowl.
5. Serve right away to your cat or keep in the fridge for up to three days.

Tips for Making Homemade Cat Food

Consult your vet: To ensure that your cat's unique nutritional requirements are being satisfied/met, it is very crucial to speak with your vet or nutritionist before producing homemade cat food.

Make use of premium ingredients: Select and use fresh, high-quality foods/ingredients devoid of any additives and preservatives.

Cats need a lot of protein in their diets or meals, so incorporate protein-rich items like chicken, turkey, beef, lamb, and fish in your recipes you choose.

Include fruits and veggies: Fruits and vegetables provide your cat the vitamins and minerals that they need for good health and growth. These consumable fruits Include foods like apples, spinach, carrots, and peas.

Be aware of portion sizes: You should give your cat the right amount of food/treats depending on their weight, age, allergy and degree of activity.

Recipe 4: Beef and Carrot Stew Cat Food

Ingredients:

One (1) pound of ground beef

One (1) cup of carrots, chopped

Chopped sweet potatoes, half a cup

½(half) cup green beans, chopped

Chopped zucchini, half a cup

Olive oil, (one) 1 tbsp.

One (1) tablespoon of dried thyme

Fourteen (14) cup finely minced fresh parsley

Instructions:

1. Olive oil should be heated slowly in a large pan over medium heat.

2. As it cooks, split up the ground beef into little pieces as you add it and cook until it is browned.
3. Stir together the sliced carrots, sweet potatoes, green beans, and zucchini in the cooking pan.
4. Bring the water in the pan to boil, and then add enough water to cover the veggies in the pan.
5. For 21~26 minutes, or until you notice the veggies are soft, reduce the heat to low and simmer.

6. Stir all together the fresh parsley that has been cut and dried thyme in the skillet.
7. Before serving, let the stew cool off, and keep any leftovers in the fridge.

Recipe 5: Beef and Carrot Meatballs Cat Food

Ingredients:

One (1) pound of ground beef

Grated carrots in a cup/bowl

0.5 cups of oats

Fourteen (14) cup finely minced fresh parsley

Olive oil, One (1) tbsp.

One (1) tablespoon dried basil

One (1) beaten egg

Instructions:

1. Set your oven's temperature to 375°F (190°C).
2. The Ground beef, shredded small carrots, oats, finely chopped fresh parsley, olive oil, and dried basil should be all combined in a large mixing dish/bowl.
3. Mix all thoroughly after adding the beaten egg to the bowl.
4. Put the mixture on a baking sheet that has been prepared out

with parchment paper and then shape it into little meatballs.
5. The meatballs should be baked in the preheated oven for 20 to 25 minutes, or until well done.
6. Before serving, let the meatballs cool, and keep any leftovers in the fridge for up to three days by storing them in an airtight container.

Turkey and Spinach recipe

Recipe 6: Turkey and Spinach Stew Cat Food

Ingredients:

One (1) pound of turkey meat

One (1) cup of spinach, chopped

Chopped carrots, half a cup

Chopped green beans, half a cup

A half-cup of chopped zucchini

One (1) teaspoon dried rosemary and 1 tablespoon olive oil

Fourteen (14) cup finely minced fresh parsley

Instructions:

1. Get a bottle of Olive oil and add to a pan , it should be heated slowly in a semi large or large pan over medium heat
2. Add a grounded turkey and heat it slowly, breaking it up as it

cooks, until it is shown browned.

3. Stir together spinach, carrots, green beans, and zucchini after adding them to the pan with olive oil.
4. Bring water to the pan to a boil, and then add enough water to cover the veggies in it.
5. Wait 18-23 minutes, or until the veggies are soft, reduce the heat to low and sieve.
6. Stir together the fresh parsley that has been cut/chopped and the dry rosemary in the skillet.

7. Before serving to your cat, let the stew cool, and keep any leftovers in the fridge in a container.

Recipe 7: Turkey and Spinach Patties Cat Food

Ingredients:

One (1) pound of turkey meat

One (1) cup of spinach, chopped

Oatmeal, half a cup, and fresh parsley, quarter a cup

Olive oil, One (1) tbsp.

One (1) tablespoon of dried thyme

One (1) beaten egg

Instructions:

1. Set the oven's temperature to 375°F (190°C).
2. Ground turkey, spinach, oats, fresh parsley, olive oil, and dried thyme combined in a large mixing basin/bowl.
3. Mix thoroughly after adding the beaten egg to the bowl used.
4. Put the mixture on a baking sheet that has been prepared and put it into tiny patties.
5. Cooked in 15-20 20 minutes in your preheated oven.
6. Once cool then serve.

Vegetarian Cat Food Recipe

Ingredients:

One (1) cup of brown rice, cooked

A half-cup of cooked lentils

½ (half) cup mashed sweet potatoes and 1/2 cup cooked quinoa

Chopped spinach, half a cup

14 cup of carrots, chopped

Green beans cut into 1/4 cup

Olive oil, 1 tbsp.

Supplemental taurine, available at pet shops, 1/4 teaspoon

Supplemental vitamin B12 is available at health food shops in 1/4 teaspoon doses.

Instructions:

1. According to the directions on the rice box, prepare the brown rice, lentils, and quinoa, then let them cool.
2. Set the oven's temperature to 375°F (190°C).
3. Combine the cooked brown rice, lentils, and quinoa with the mashed sweet potato, spinach, carrots, green beans, and olive oil in a large bowl.
4. Blend well.

5. Mix thoroughly before adding the taurine (supplement) and vitamin B12 pills.
6. Put the mixture on a baking sheet and put it into tiny patties.
7. The patties cooked through after 20~25 minutes in the preheated oven.
8. Before serving, let the patties cool

CHAPTER 6: ADVANCED HOMEMADE CAT FOOD RECIPES

Recipe 1: *Pâté with chicken and liver*

Ingredients:

One (1) pound of skinless, boneless chicken thighs

One (1) pound of washed chicken liver

Olive oil and one(1) cup of chicken broth

Dried rosemary, One (1) teaspoon

One teaspoon dried thyme

One (1)-tablespoon-dried parsley

Apple cider vinegar, One (1) tablespoon

A tablespoon of basic yogurt

Instructions:

1. Turn the oven on to 375(°F).
2. Chicken thighs, liver, chicken broth, extra virgin olive oil, dried rosemary, dried thyme, and dried parsley too should be all combined in a big dish.
3. Put all the ingredients in a large baking dish after thoroughly combining and stirring them.
4. Bake the mixture for 44–51 minutes, or until the liver is

seen soft and the chicken is well cooked.

5. After taking the dish out of the oven, let it cool off a little.
6. Transfer the mixture made to a food processor, and process it in short bursts until it resembles pâté.
7. Once more pulse until well blended before adding the yogurt and apple cider vinegar (if you using this).
8. You may either serve right away to your cat or keep the food in the fridge.

Recipe 2: Tuna and rice bowl

Ingredients:

Two (2) drained tuna in water cans

One (1) cup of brown rice, cooked

50 ml of boiled peas

Chopped half a cup of cooked carrots

14 cup finely minced fresh parsley

One (1)-tablespoon olive oil

A teaspoon of dried catnip

Instructions:

1. Tuna, brown rice, peas, carrots, parsley, olive oil, and catnip (if these used) should all be combined in a big dish.
2. Then combine the components.

3. The combination may be consumed right once or kept in the fridge for up to three days after it is done.

Recipe 3: Beef and vegetable stew

Ingredients:

One (1) pound of lean ground beef

One (1) cup of carrots, chopped

Green beans and sweet potatoes, each cup diced

One (1) cup of spinach, chopped

Two (2) tbsp. olive oil and 1 cup water

One (1) teaspoon dried thyme

One (1) teaspoon dried oregano

Instructions:

1. Olive oil should be heated slowly in a large saucepan over a medium-high heat.
2. Brown the ground beef after adding it up.
3. Green beans, spinach, carrots, and sweet potatoes then diced and added to the stew.
4. Water, dried thyme, and dried oregano added after thoroughly combining the ingredients used.
5. The mixture should be brought to a boil before being simmered for 30-40 minutes, depending

on how tender you want your veggies to be.

6. Then give the stew for consuming.

To make sure the recipe you are using satisfies and meets your cat's specific nutritional needs, you must speak with a veterinarian or veterinary nutritionist before producing any homemade cat food for consumption. Gently introduce any new meals you want to give and keep a careful eye on your cat's health and behavior.

Homemade cat treats

Recipe one; Tuna and catnip treats

Ingredients:

-One (1) can of drained tuna in water

One (1) egg, 1/2 cup oat flour, and 1 tablespoon dried catnip

Instructions:

1. Set the oven's temperature to 350(°F).

2. Combine the tuna fish, egg, oat flour, and dried catnip in a medium bowl.

3. Scoop out little balls of the mixture and set them on a baking sheet covered with parchment paper.

4. Bake the goodies for 10-15 minutes, or until they are firm and golden brown.

5. Before serving to your cat, let the desserts cool fully.

Recipe 2: Sweet potato with chicken treats

Ingredients

One (1) lb of cooked then shredded boneless and skinless chicken breasts

- 1/four-cup oat flour - 1/4 cup water - 1/2 cup mashed sweet potato

Instructions:

1. Set the oven's temperature to 350(°F).
2. Combine the shredded chicken, mashed sweet potato, oat flour, and water in a large or semi large bowl.
3. Scoop out tiny balls or patties of the mixture made and arrange them on a baking sheet covered with parchment paper.
4. Bake the goodies for 18-20 minutes, or until they are firm and golden brown.
5. Then serve, let the desserts cool fully.

Recipe 3: Pumpkin and Salmon Treats

Ingredients

One (1) can of flakes salmon in water, 1 egg, 1/2 cup pumpkin puree, 1/4 cup coconut flour, and One(1) can of flaked salmon.

Instructions:

1. Set the oven's temperature to 340°F.
2. Combine flaked salmon, pumpkin puree, coconut flour, and egg in a medium bowl.

3. Scoop out little balls of the mixture and set them on a baking sheet covered with parchment paper.
4. Bake the goodies for 15-20 minutes, or until they are firm and golden brown.
5. Cool off then serve

Recipe 4: Beef and carrot jerky

Ingredients: One (1) lb. thinly sliced lean meat; one (1) cup grated carrots.

- One (1) tsp. dried parsley – Two (2) tbsp. coconut oil

Instructions:

1. Set the oven's temperature to 175(°F).
2. Combine the beef strips, grated carrots, coconut oil, and dried parsley in a semi or large bowl.
3. Arrange the beef strips on a parchment-lined baking sheet.
4. Bake the jerky for 3[three] to 4[four] hours, or until it is crisp and dry.
5. Always cool off then serve.

Recipe 5; Turkey and cranberry bites

Ingredients: One (1) pound ground turkey; 1/2 cup minced dried cranberries.

- One (1) egg ~ 1/4 cup oat flour

Instructions:

1. Set the oven's temperature to 350(°F).
2. Combine the grounded turkey, finely chopped dried cranberries, oat flour, and egg in a medium basin/bowl.
3. Scoop out little balls of the mixture made and set them on a baking sheet covered with parchment paper.
4. Bake the goodies for 20-25 minutes, or until they are firm and golden brown.

5. Once done and brown then serve to your cat

CHAPTER 7

Special Diet Cat Food (for allergies, kidney disease, etc.)

For some cats with certain medical concerns including allergies, renal illness, or diabetes, special diet cat food is very crucial to be added for their health. These diets are designed and prepared to provide the best nourishment while also assisting in the management of the condition's symptoms of their illness. The following recipes are suggested and advised for cats with various medical conditions:

- **Cat food recipe that's allergy-friendly**

Ingredients: One (1) pound of cooked ground turkey; One (1) of cup mashed sweet potatoes; 1/2 cup mashed fruit carrots; 1/2 cup chopped green beans and one(1) tablespoon olive oil.

- 1/2 tsp of dried oregano and 1(one) teaspoon dried parsley

Instructions:

1. In a pan, sauté [fry quickly] the ground turkey until it is totally done.
2. Combine the cooked turkey, mashed sweet potatoes, mashed fruit carrots, diced green beans, olive oil, dried parsley, and dried oregano in a large dish or bowl.
3. Before serving to your cat, allow the mixture to cool.

Cats that are allergic to typical proteins like chicken or beef should try more of this dish. It offers a healthy, well-balanced supper to them with a variety of protein sources.

- **Cat Food for Kidney Disease:**

Ingredient

One (1) pound. ground pork, 1/2 cup cooked brown rice, 1/2 cup cooked peas, 1/4 cup chopped carrots, and 1/4 cup chopped green beans are the ingredients.

One (1) tablespoon of fish oil with- 1/4 teaspoon each of salt and potassium chloride

Instructions:

1. In a pan, sauté [quickly fried] the ground pork until it is totally done.

2. Combine the cooked pork, with brown rice, peas, diced carrots, chopped green beans, fish oil, salt, and potassium chloride in a large dish or bowl.
3. Then serve, Before serving, allow the mixture you made to cool before giving your cat.

This recipe's minimal protein, salt, and phosphorus content in it makes it the perfect choice for cats that have renal illness or symptoms.

- **Cat Diabetic Food:**

Ingredients:

One (1) pound of ground beef, 1/2 cup of cooked quinoa, and 1/2 cup of chopped, cooked broccoli as veggies.

- 1/two cup chopped, cooked zucchini

One (1)-tablespoon coconut oil

- 1/4 tsp. cinnamon and one (1) teaspoon dried basil

Instructions:

1. In a pan, sauté the ground beef until it is totally done enough.
2. Combine your cooked meat, cooked quinoa, finely chopped broccoli, finely chopped zucchini, coconut oil, dried

basil, and cinnamon in a large bowl or basil for them.

3. Then serve Warm

Due to this food high fiber content and low carbohydrate content, this dish is perfect for diabetic cats. Quinoa, which is included in this meal, serves as a rich source of both complex carbs and protein.

CHAPTER 8; FEEDING GUIDELINES AND TIPS

How much homemade cat food to feed

The quantity of homemade cat food you should give your pet cat will vary depending on a number of variables, including your cat's age, weight, level of activity shown, and general health. Working closely with your doctor or a veterinary nutritionist can help you choose the right quantity of food to give your cat based on their specific requirements or needs.

An adult cat that is quite healthy should generally ingest 23-34 calories per pound of body weight each day. A 15-pound cat, for instance, would need 245–355 calories per day. However, this may change according on the particular requirements stated of your cat or for your cat.

Keep a close eye on your cats weight while implementing these meals to them and give quantities which is necessary to make sure they are holding proper weight

TIP; Feeding your cat too little might result in malnutrition, while feeding too much of food can cause obesity and other health issues so get to balance it up with proportions.

Aside from that, it is quite crucial to give your pet cat numerous smaller meals throughout the day rather than one huge one. By doing this practice, you may avoid any intestinal discomfort and preserve a constant level of energy in them throughout the day.

Always get advice and consult a doctor or veterinary nutritionist to establish how much homemade cat food to give your cat depending on their specific requirements, health or needs.

How often to feed

Establishing a feeding regimen/routine that satisfies your cat's nutritional demands and works with your lifestyle is essential especially when it comes to feeding and preparing homemade cat food. Adult cats typically need two [2]-three [3] short meals each day, although kittens may need to be fed more often as well.

The precise feeding schedule created will vary depending on their age, weight, activity, and general health of your pet cat. For instance, a young, energetic cat/kitten need to be fed more often than an older, less active cat.

Mixing homemade cat food with commercial cat food

In order to make sure your cat is receiving all the necessary nutrients from all ends, you mix homemade cat food made with commercial cat food bought.

To balance out the homemade diet you give them, buy a premium commercial cat food to add up. A commercial cat feed manufactured with high-quality ingredients and free of additives, fillers, and artificial preservatives in it is what you should seek for in it.

Gradually combine the homemade cat food with store-bought cat food then Over the course of many weeks, gradually increase the quantity of homemade food you mix with your cat's regular commercially bought food.

Getting all the nutrients, they require to always having access to fresh water, as it is important when feeding a homemade diet that might contain less water than commercial cat feed.

Common mistakes to avoids

There are certain common errors that we all prompt to make which should be avoided when creating homemade cat food in order to guarantee that your cat is eating a diet that is both nutritionally full for them and balanced. Here are some typical errors/mistakes to avoid when making your homemade cat food:

1. Omitting all vital nutrients: Omitting any critical needed nutrients that cats need for good health is one of the major blunders individuals always make when creating homemade cat food. To make sure that your homemade cat food has all of the vital nutrients your cat need, like protein, fat, vitamins,

minerals, and amino acids, see a nutritionist

2. Feeding your pet cat excessively or insufficiently might result in health issues, such as obesity and malnutrition.
3. Not adhering to instructions or recipes[make research before adding your thought through ingredient]
4. Making homemade cat food using poor-quality ingredients/ materials
5. Improper food storage

Follow basic food Safety

Fundamental food safety principles.

1. Prior to and during their food preparation, properly wash your hands and clean all tools and surfaces used.
2. Use premium components that are hygienic for their consumption and fresh. **Do not** use ingredients that have gone bad or have expired.
3. Thoroughly cook meat well and fish to remove any

potentially hazardous germs or parasites in it.

4. To avoid cross-contamination from tools, use distinct cutting surfaces and tools for meat and other components used.

5. To avoid any bacterial development and deterioration, store your homemade cat food in sealed containers in the freezer or refrigerator to stay fresh over time.

6. Never keep homemade cat food at room temperature;

always use the microwave or refrigerator to warm or store.

7. After 2[two]-3[three] days in the fridge or two [2]-three [3] months in the freezer, dispose of any uneaten homemade food.

Size matters

Making your homemade cat food requires taking the cat's size into account and consideration since it influences the nutritional needs and portion sizes.

1. **Portion sizes**: Cats come in a variety of sizes, and the amount of food they should eat or given to them will depend on their size, weight, and degree of activity. In general, bigger cats need greater serving sizes than smaller cats.

2. **Dietary needs**: Cats that are larger have different dietary needs than cats that are smaller. Larger cats need more protein and calories to keep their weight and energy levels stable to smaller cat on size and portion,

3. Texture: The texture of the homemade cat food you gibe will

vary depending on the size of your cat's mouth and teeth. Take an instance, if your cat has little teeth, it could find it challenging to chew through big pieces of meat so to make the meat simpler for your cat to consume in this situation, you may need to ground or puree it to their side.

CHAPTER 7: TIPS FOR TRANSITION

Getting your cat to love Homemade food

It may take some time, practice and work to get your cat to like and transit homemade food, but it will be worthwhile for their health and welfare of your pet cat. The following advice can make your cat like homemade food:

1. Introduce the homemade meal gradually to them, blending it first with their usual diet that they are

used. Your cat will be able to adjust to the new flavor and texture without feeling overwhelmed if you do this practice.

2. Use premium ingredients: Give your cat's senses something tasty and enticing by using premium, fresh foods/ingredients. As carnivores, cats tend to need a lot of protein from meat or fish in their diets or meals.

3. Experiment with tastes and textures: Because cats can be fussy eaters, it is vital to see what your pet cat enjoys by trying out various flavors and textures of food. For

instance, certain cats can like fish over chicken/turkey or ground meat over pieces.

4. Include variation in your cat's diet, by rotating various homemade recipes you made or include some healthy snacks in it will not get your cat tired of eating the same thing every day.

5. Serve food at the proper temperature. Some cats enjoy their food cold, while others want it slightly warmed up so therefore try different serving temperatures to see which ones your cat likes/prefers most.

6. Make meals pleasurable and enjoyable for your cat: Try to make their mealtime enjoyable for your cat to establish a good link with it.

Remember that every cat is unique in their own way, so it could take some trial and error in thus practice to figure out what suits your cat the best. As time goes, your cat will ultimately develop a taste for your homemade food if you are persistent and patient with them.

Getting your cat used to home-cooked meals

To prevent disturbing your cat's digestive system while switching your cat from store-bought [commercial food] food to homemade food, it is necessary to make the switch gradual and steady. The following advice can help you get your cat used to eating homemade food:

1. Take it gently at first. Start by blending a tiny quantity of their homemade food with your cat's usual food. Over the course of seven [7]-ten [10] days, then gradually increase the amount of food you give them as this will enable the digestive system of

your pet cat to gradually become used to the new diet given to them.

2. Keep an eye on your cat's appetite: Keep a careful eye on your cat's appetite throughout the changeover of diet. You may need to take your time making the transition happen or try a new dish or recipe if they are not eating as much as they usually do.

3. Keep an eye out for digestive problems: Look out for symptoms of digestive problems such as diarrhea, vomiting, or constipation. Stop the transition immediately if you detect

any of these signs mentioned, and speak with your veterinarian.

4. Gently reduce the quantity of commercial food you given until your cat is just eating homemade food. Once your cat is comfortable eating the homemade food without any problems, gently reduce the amount of commercial food as well.

5. Ensure sufficient nutrition: Consult a doctor or veterinary nutritionist to get advice/make sure, the homemade food you are giving your cat satisfies the dietary requirements.

6. Maintain consistency: It is important to continue feeding your cat homemade food once they have successfully made the switch or transition. Do not introduce any new meals or make abrupt sudden adjustments without first contacting your veterinarian.

Veteran transition consultant

Consulting is an essential step in converting your cat from commercial to homemade meals made ,A veterinarian can provide advice on the changeover process you are taking and to help check that your cat's nutritional requirements are being satisfied.

A veterinarian will help you in the following ways as you make the transition:

1. Examine your cat's medical past.
2. Offer dietary advice
3. Make supplement recommendations
4. Track your cat's development

5. Continued help: A vet can provide support and direction during the food transition as well as respond to any queries you may have about your cat's food and nutrition as time goes.

Tip: Making the switch from store-bought to homemade cat food is quite a significant decision that is strongly encouraged.

CONCLUSION: MAKING HOMEMADE CAT FOOD FOR HEALTHIER, HAPPIER CATS

Making your own cat food is an excellent method to provide your cat a balanced diet that is very healthy and will enhance their general health and happiness. Also, make sure your cat is getting all the proper nutrients they need to flourish by using high-quality fresh ingredients and following a balanced formula.

Even while switching your cat to a homemade food the experience can be enjoyable for both you and your pet cat. To make sure that your cat's nutritional requirements are being fulfilled/met and to track their development during the meal transition, *remember* to always check with a veterinarian or veterinary nutritionist.

You can provide your cat a diet that promotes their health and happiness and deepens the link between you and your feline buddy with a little time and effort put into this practice.

THE END...GOODLUCK

NOTES;

Printed in Great Britain
by Amazon